WITHDRAWN

HOW TO IMPROVE AT PLAYING
GUITAR

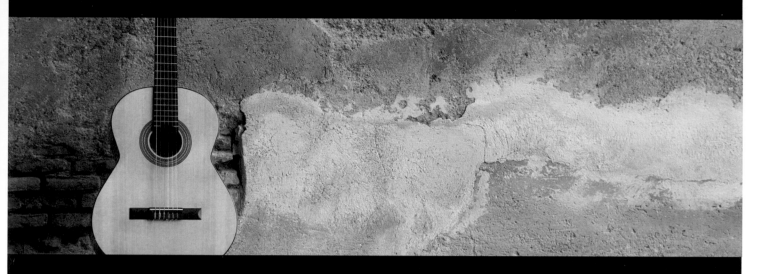

Tom Clark

 Crabtree Publishing Company

www.crabtreebooks.com

MAR 2013

Author: Tom Clark
Editor: Dan Green
Consultant editor: Mark Eden
Proofreader: Marion Dent
Editorial director: Kathy Middleton
Designer: Christine Lacey
Indexer: Michael Dent
Prepress technician: Margaret Amy Salter
Production coordinator: Margaret Amy Salter
Production controller: Ed Green
Production manager: Suzy Kelly

Produced by dangEditions
All music copyright © TickTock Entertainment Ltd 2010

Photo credits:
All photographs by Andy Crawford except:

Shutterstock: title page, p.2, p.3 (top left), p.3, p.4 (top left and middle),
    p.6 (middle right), p.13 (middle right), p.18 (top right), p.19 (bottom
    right), p.21 (bottom right), p.28 (bottom right), p.29 (middle right),
    p.36 (top right), p.42 (top right)
iStockphoto: p.8 (top right), p.10 (bottom right), p.33 (top left and middle
    right), p.38 (top right)
Rex Images: p.45 (bottom left and right), p.46, p.47 (top right, bottom left)
Getty Images: p.44, p.45 (top left), p.47 (middle and bottom right)
All exercises and melodies by Tom Clark, except Malagueña (Trad. p.20),
    Scarborough Fair (Trad. p.23), Traditional Irish Tune (Trad. p.35)

The publisher would like to thank Junior Guildhall for their help in the
production of this book. In particular: Derek Rodgers, Alison Mears, and
James Wilson. Guildhall Students: William Arnold-Forster, Johan Clubb,
Danisha Cochrane, Andreas Hogstrand, Zara Hudson-Kozdoj, Marie Luc,
Mario Marin-Borquez, Michael Oram, Chantal Osindero, Umi Pawlyn,
Philip Protheroe, Anshuman Sinha, Torrin Williams

Library and Archives Canada Cataloguing in Publication

Clark, Tom, 1965-
    How to improve at playing guitar / Tom Clark.

(How to improve at--)
Includes index.
ISBN 978-0-7787-3578-6 (bound).--ISBN 978-0-7787-3600-4 (pbk.)

1. Guitar--Instruction and study--Juvenile.
I. Title. II. Series: How to improve at--

MT801.G8C595 2010   787.87'193   C2009-907429-X

Library of Congress Cataloging-in-Publication Data

Clark, Tom, 1965-
 How to improve at playing guitar / Tom Clark.
    p. cm. -- (How to improve at--)
 Includes index.
 ISBN 978-0-7787-3600-4 (pbk. : alk. paper) -- ISBN 978-0-7787-3578-6
(reinforced library binding : alk. paper)
 1. Guitar--Instruction and study--Juvenile. I. Title. II. Series.

 MT801.G8C53 2010
 787.87'193--dc22
                                                        2009051338

Crabtree Publishing Company

www.crabtreebooks.com   1-800-387-7650

Published in Canada
Crabtree Publishing
616 Welland Ave.
St. Catharines, Ontario
L2M 5V6

Published in the United States
Crabtree Publishing
PMB 59051
350 Fifth Avenue, 59ᵗʰ Floor
New York, New York 10118

Printed in the U.S.A./012010/BG20091216

CONTENTS

2

INTRODUCTION

The guitar is the world's most popular instrument. It's portable and can be used for a vast range of musical styles. This book will help you improve your playing, from learning the basics to writing melodies. In the words of country music songwriter Harlan Howard, all you need is "three chords and the truth."

A BIT OF HISTORY

The origins of the guitar are lost in the mists of time, but one thing is for sure—it was adapted from older instruments, such as the Moroccan "oud" and the Scandinavian "lute." The earliest guitars first appeared around 1600 and had 10 strings arranged in five pairs. Steel-string acoustic guitars were first developed in the 1800s and the first electric guitars were built in the 1940s.

HOW TO USE THIS BOOK

You can work through the book page-by-page, or leap ahead to learn about a particular skill or to practice playing some exercises. Step-by-step guides show you proper technique, and the exercises help you practice them.

Top tip boxes

Watch for these helpful boxes, which will give you a lot of juicy extras, including top tips on technique, and explanations of the terms, signs, and symbols used in guitar playing and music.

THE GUITAR

Before you start playing, let's get to know your instrument. A guitar is not complicated. Even though there are many different types of guitars, they all share the same basic working parts.

THE GUITAR FAMILY

Not counting banjos, ukeleles, mandolins, and all the other instruments in the family, there is a mind-boggling variety of guitars. Luckily, they divide neatly into two different types—acoustic guitars and electric guitars.

Guitar varieties

Acoustic guitars all make sound in the same way—when you pluck a string, the sound is amplified, or made louder, inside the hollow body of the guitar. Classical guitars have nylon strings and wide fretboards and are ideal guitars for beginners. Steel-string guitars have narrower, curved fretboards and use steel strings. Classical guitars are mostly used to play classical and Spanish flamenco music, while steel-string guitars can be used in many styles including folk, jazz, and rock music.

Electric guitars use a device called a pickup to amplify the sound. Because they don't rely on a hollow body to create their sound, they are often solid-bodied (*see* below).

Going Electric

Electric guitars use pickups to make their sound. Pickups convert the vibration of the steel strings into electrical signals. Unplugged, an electric guitar doesn't make much noise, but you can make a much, much louder sound when you play it through an amplifier. Amplifiers take the weak signals from the pickups and can boost them to ear-splitting levels.

Effects Pedals

Effects pedals are electronic circuits that change the way the guitar sounds. The distortion pedal adds volume and crunch, while the delay pedal makes many repeating echoes.

Guitar Cable

As well as an amplifier, the one other piece of equipment essential for playing the electric guitar is a cable. This cord connects the guitar to the amplifier— no cable, no sound.

PARTS OF A GUITAR

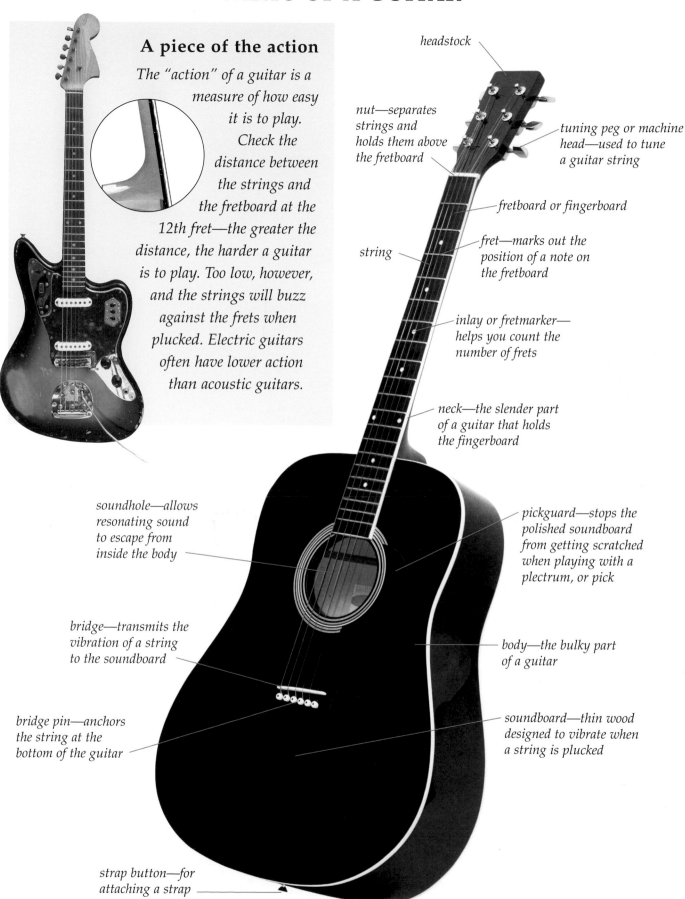

A piece of the action

The "action" of a guitar is a measure of how easy it is to play. Check the distance between the strings and the fretboard at the 12th fret—the greater the distance, the harder a guitar is to play. Too low, however, and the strings will buzz against the frets when plucked. Electric guitars often have lower action than acoustic guitars.

headstock

nut—separates strings and holds them above the fretboard

tuning peg or machine head—used to tune a guitar string

fretboard or fingerboard

string

fret—marks out the position of a note on the fretboard

inlay or fretmarker—helps you count the number of frets

neck—the slender part of a guitar that holds the fingerboard

soundhole—allows resonating sound to escape from inside the body

pickguard—stops the polished soundboard from getting scratched when playing with a plectrum, or pick

bridge—transmits the vibration of a string to the soundboard

body—the bulky part of a guitar

bridge pin—anchors the string at the bottom of the guitar

soundboard—thin wood designed to vibrate when a string is plucked

strap button—for attaching a strap

TUNING

Before you can play anything on your guitar, you must tune it. Each string is tuned to a specific note so that the guitar doesn't sound jarring and off-key when you play it.

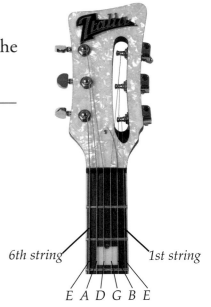

STANDARD TUNING

The usual tuning for a guitar is, from 6th string to 1st string (*see* opposite page): E, A, D, G, B, E. This is called standard tuning, and a good way to remember it is with the silly sentence, "Edward And David Grow Big Elephants."

6th string   1st string

E A D G B E

TUNING TO SOMETHING

Guitars can be tuned to themselves, so that each string sounds in tune with the others. But to play with other people, you must tune all the instruments to the same note. An electronic tuner is the easiest way to do this. It detects the sound of each individual string and tells you whether it's in tune or not. Some tuners even tell you which way to turn the tuning peg to get a string in tune.

Technical terms

pitch—The "lowness" or "highness" of a guitar string, or note

`Electronic tuner`

HOW TO TUNE UP

Every string is wound around a tuning peg (for classical guitars) or machine head (for steel-string guitars). To adust the tuning, these are turned to make the string tighter (making the pitch higher) or looser (making the pitch lower). It's always good to check your tuning before playing because strings can go out of tune quickly.

SIMPLE TUNING METHOD

Tune your 6th string using an electronic tuner or another instrument that is in tune. Then use your 6th string to tune the rest of the strings.

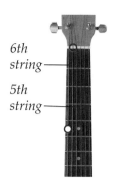

6th string
5th string

STEP 1

Play an A on the 5th fret of the 6th string. Now play the open 5th string, and turn the tuning peg until it is in tune with the A on the 6th string.

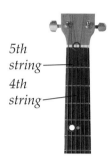

5th string
4th string

STEP 2

Play a D note on the 5th fret of the 5th string. Play the open 4th string and match the sounds.

Top tip

It's always easier to tune up to a note than tuning down. Don't give up if it is hard at first—tuning takes practice.

STEP 3

Repeat the process playing a G on the 5th fret of the 4th string and the open 3rd string.

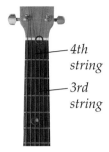

4th string
3rd string

STEP 4

This time play a B note on the 4th fret of the 3rd string and compare it to the open 2nd string.

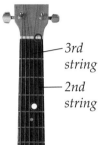

3rd string
2nd string

STEP 5

Finally, the 5th fret of the 2nd string will give you another E note, to which you can tune the open 1st string.

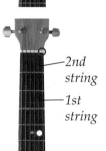

2nd string
1st string

PLAYING POSITIONS

Learning a good playing position helps you relax and snag those hard-to-reach notes.

There are two main ways of holding a guitar. A folk style has the guitar resting on your leg on the same side as your strumming or picking hand. In this position the neck is horizontal. In a classical playing style, the guitar rests on the opposite knee to the plucking hand. The neck slopes upwards in this position. Many players use a footstool to make it more comfortable.

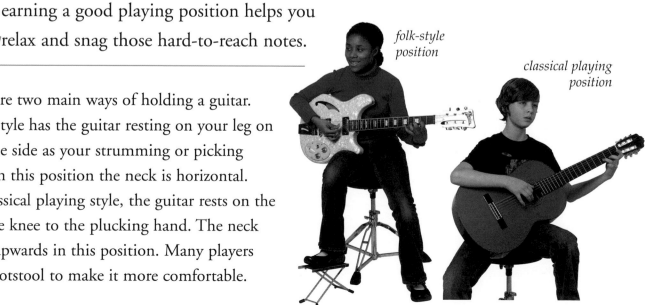

folk-style position

classical playing position

STRUMMING AND PICKING

To make any sound on a guitar, you need to pluck the strings. You can do this one at a time, which is called picking, or all together, which is called **strumming**. Now get ready to raise the roof!

STRUMMING TECHNIQUE

STEP 1

You can strum with your fingers or use a small plastic triangle called a plectrum, more commonly known as a pick. Plucking the strings with a pick makes a strong, clear and even tone. Grip it loosely between thumb and index finger, and point it in toward the guitar's body.

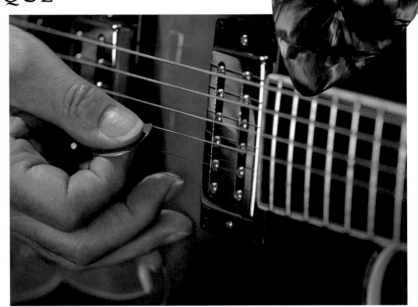

STEP 2

Your elbow should rest comfortably on the guitar with your hand off the strings.

STEP 3

Gently brush the pick down across the strings. Hit each string cleanly one at a time.

STEP 4

Make sure to strum midway between the bridge and the top of the body. This makes the loudest sound.

Strumming in a downward direction from the 6th string to the 1st string is called a downstroke.

STEP 5

The upstroke is the reverse of the downstroke.

STEP 6

Start slowly and concentrate on accuracy before building up speed.

Strumming in an upward direction from the 1st string to the 6th string is called an upstroke.

Top tip

When it comes to strumming, the harder you strum the worse it sounds. Make sure you brush the strings gently and evenly.

PLAYING P-I-M-A

Classical guitar is played by plucking individual strings with the thumb or a finger. The thumb plays downward, while the fingers push through the string and in toward the palm of the hand. Do not pull the strings outward. In classical guitar, each playing digit is given a letter. The thumb is "P," the 1st finger is "I," the 2nd finger is "M," and the 3rd finger is "A." This labeling system allows a composer to show the picking pattern on a piece of music.

Classical strokes

There are two types of finger strokes in the classical right-hand technique. Apoyando, or rest stroke, produces a fuller, more singing and projected tone, suitable for melodic lines. Tirando, or free stroke, is used for more intricate plucking patterns. With apoyando, the thumb or finger comes to rest on the next-door string. With tirando, the finger or thumb finishes above the strings.

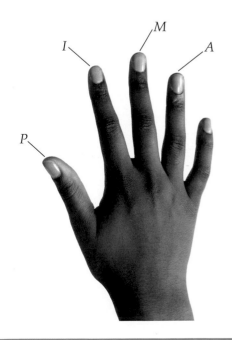

MUSICAL NOTATION

Guitar has its own special method for writing down music, called tablature. "Tab" is really quick and easy to read, but it's also worth learning how to read standard notation—what you might call "reading music."

HOW TAB WORKS

In tablature, each line represents a string on your guitar. The numbers correspond to the fret number on the fingerboard.

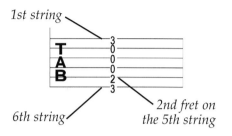

1st string

6th string

2nd fret on the 5th string

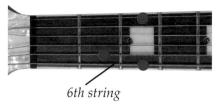

6th string

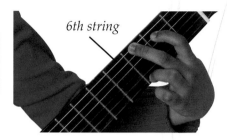

6th string

STEP 1

This is tab for the chord of G major. When the numbers are in a vertical line, it means play them all together.

STEP 2

The tab lines represent the strings of the guitar and show you which frets to finger.

STEP 3

The player's fingers match the positions shown on the tab.

STEP 4

When the notes of a chord are staggered, it means they are each played separately, as an **arpeggio**.

STEP 5

Single-note sequences are written one after the other, reading from left to right.

STANDARD NOTATION

In standard notation, notes are written on a staff. Every note on a guitar fretboard has its own unique place on the staff. Standard notation is better for showing more complex rhythms and finger plucking than tablature.

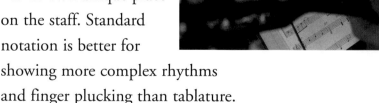

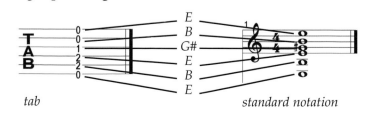

tab

standard notation

PRACTICE PIECES

Practice reading tablature and playing along with the three examples below. Once you have got the hang of tab, try to get a feel for how the notes on the staff match to the fret positions on your guitar. Test yourself by covering the tab with a piece of paper to see if you can still play along. Remember to start off playing slowly before building up speed.

BLUES SCALES EXERCISE

This exercise uses notes from the blues scale (*see* page 36).

EXERCISE 11.1

MAJOR PENTATONIC EXERCISE

You will find the major pentatonic scale in its entirety on page 38.

EXERCISE 11.2

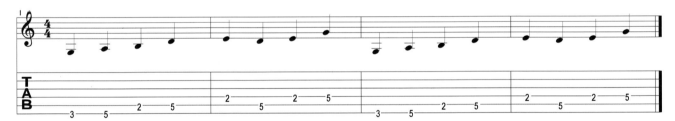

MINOR PENTATONIC EXERCISE

The minor pentatonic scale is often used by rock guitarists when they play solos. Here is an exercise based on notes from the minor pentatonic scale (*see* page 39).

EXERCISE 11.3

WARMING UP

Just like any athlete, if you want to perform well, you're going to have to warm up first. Here are some tips and tricks to get your blood pumping.

Practice clever

Warming up before playing is very important. As well as loosening the fingers, it gets you focused and ready for whatever you need to do. Here are some tips for warming up:
- *Begin your practice with slow and rhythmic playing, giving your fingers a chance to warm up gradually.*
- *Pick different warm-up exercises for each practice.*
- *Once you can play the warm-ups, challenge yourself to play them faster. Try them out both **staccato** and **legato** (see page 27).*

BLUES SCALES EXERCISE

This blues scale is in the key of G major. This means it is based around the notes in the chord of G (right).

G

EXERCISE 12.1

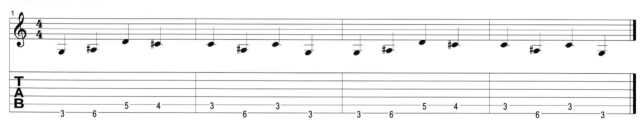

UP THE NECK IN OCTAVES

Try this ascending **octaves** exercise to build up your speed, agility, and accuracy. Keep the notes clean and even.

EXERCISE 12.2

MY OWN WARM-UP EXERCISE

I use this exercise to warm up before going on stage. The note length gets shorter in the final two bars—it speeds up, but the notes stay evenly spaced.

Try this warm-up routine. It starts on the 7th fret of the 6th string, which is a B note (shown left).

EXERCISE 13.1

March to the beat

Keep a steady pace by playing your exercises along with a **metronome**. *Play each new note with every click. Start off at about 50 beats per minute (BPM). Once you feel comfortable, move it up to 60 BPM, and so on.*

This is another single-note sequence, which ends on a D note—5th fret on the 5th string (*see* right). Notice how the different note values (how long each note lasts) affect the rhythm (*see* page 18).

EXERCISE 13.2

OPEN CHORDS

Chords are combinations of two or more notes played at the same time. **Open chords** use the tuning of the open, or unfretted, guitar strings to create chiming sounds. A small number of chords can unlock many songs.

CHORD CHARTS

When playing chords, try to keep a good hand position. Plant your thumb firmly on the middle of the neck, round your hand, and press your fingers down squarely on the frets.

MAJOR CHORDS

Chords that are made from the major scale have a happy feel. This is because the intervals, or gaps, between the notes in the major scale always make the perfect harmonic, or pure tone, sound.

Chords at your fingertips

Use these pages as a chord dictionary. You can flip back to them any time you need to remember a certain chord shape.

E MAJOR

E major is made up of the notes E, B, E, G#, B, and E. Play all six strings together.

A MAJOR

A major is formed from the notes A, E, A, C#, and E. Make sure to play only strings 1 to 5.

D MAJOR

D major uses only the strings 1 to 4. It's made up of the notes D, A, D, and F#.

G MAJOR

You can play all six strings for G major. The chord uses the notes G, B, D, G, B, and G.

C MAJOR

*Be careful to tuck your 4th finger out of the way to avoid **deadening** the 1st string.*

F MAJOR

The chord of F major requires the 1st finger to fret the 1st fret on both the 1st and 2nd strings.

MINOR CHORDS

Based on the notes of the minor scales, minor chords have a sad, melancholic feel. Try playing a major chord of any key, followed by a minor chord in the same key to hear the difference.

Roots and tonics

*A chord is made up of a combination of notes from the scale in that key. For example, E major chord is made of notes from the E major scale. The first note of the scale is called the **tonic**. In most open chords the root note, or the lowest note, is also the tonic.*

15

E MINOR (Em)

The notes E, B, E, G, B, and E make up the chord of E minor, which is played on all six strings.

A MINOR (Am)

As with all minor chords, the A minor is made by dropping the third note in the scale by a semitone (a half tone, or one fret).

Super strength

The more you play, the stronger your fingers will get. With practice, your muscles will get stronger, your fingers will toughen up, and your chords will sound much better for it.

D MINOR (Dm)

D minor is played on strings 1 to 4—the notes of D, A, D, and F.

SEVENTH CHORDS

Seventh chords are a special group of chords that, along with the notes of the major or minor scale, also have an added dominant seventh. This is the seventh note in the scale and is a whole tone, or two frets down, from the root note, or tonic (*see* box, page 15).

E7

Lifting the 3rd finger when playing an E major chord gives you an E7. Also try fretting the 3rd finger on the 2nd string.

A7

Seventh chords have a cool, bluesy feel. Try playing A major and following it up with an A7.

G7

The fingering of G7 is quite different from G major. Try fretting the 1st-string G with your 4th finger to make a swift change.

C7

The seventh note in the C major scale is easily dropped in to the chord of C major.

D7

 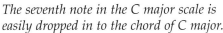

Like all D open chords, D7 is only played on strings 1 to 4. D7 is made up of D, A, C, and F#.

Clean chords

Avoid buzzing notes by pressing down on the strings as hard as you can and getting close up to the fret.

Am7

Am7 is made by lifting up the 3rd finger. You can try the same trick to turn an E minor into an Em7.

Dm7

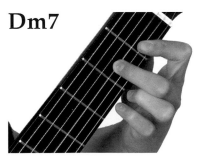 

The Dm7 chord, like F major, is played with a half-barre on the top two strings, made with the 1st finger.

BASIC SKILLS

CHORDS AND SINGLE NOTES

By now, you have excelled at plucking and strumming with a pick, and mastered fretting open chords. Now it's time to try combining the two.

THE IMPORTANCE OF PRACTICE

An essential skill for any guitar player is the ability to move smoothly between chords and single notes. Once you master the technique, you can strum out rhythm, accompaniment, and solo melody lines, as well as intricate **fills** and **riffs** to spice up your solid chord foundation.

The only way of making sure that your playing flows properly, is to spend as much time as you can practicing the techniques on your guitar.

In this exercise, a bar of chords is followed by two bars of melody line. Try your best to "flow" smoothly from the chords to the single-note movement. Imagine switching lanes on a road—keep the same speed as you shoot off in another direction without braking.

EXERCISE 17.1

Here is a similar exercise in the key of G major (based around the chord and scale of G major). The changes happen a little more often in this piece. Look out for the chord rhythms.

EXERCISE 17.2

CHORDS AND SINGLE NOTES

RHYTHM

Rhythm is at the heart of all music—it is the beat that keeps a song rolling along and sets your foot tappin'. It can be complex. At the root of every rhythm are notes and beats of varying lengths.

YOU GOT RHYTHM

The secret to good rhythm is knowing your note values. Different notes last for different lengths of time (*see* right). One of the big advantages that standard musical notation has over tablature is that it is much easier to show the rhythm you play—that's why we have included both forms for you in this book. So let's give note values a try!

Note values

o   *whole note = 4 beats*

half note = 2 beats

quarter note = 1 beat

eighth note = ½ beat

sixteenth note = ¼ beat

dotted half note = 3 beats

dotted quarter note = 1½ beats

dotted eighth note = ¾ beats

STEP 1

Clap this rhythm first (see above). Pay close attention to the length of each note.

STEP 2

If whole melodies were written out in one long line, it would get pretty confusing, so notes are grouped into bars. Each bar contains the same number of beats. Practice clapping the rhythm above.

TIME SIGNATURES

Nothing could be more important to rhythm-keeping than **time signatures**. That is why they are put right at the start of any piece of music. Time signatures tell you how many beats in a bar and how many notes per measure.

The top number shows how many beats are in the bar.

The bottom number shows what type of beat it is. A "4" means it is a quarter note, and an "8" means it is an eighth note.

Lessons

Lessons are not essential—you can teach yourself an awful lot by using books such as this one. However, it is sometimes very helpful to have personal attention to help you get through problems. A guitar teacher can give you a push when you might give up, plus it is always great to play with other people!

4/4 TIME SIGNATURE

In a bar of 4/4, there are four quarter beats in every bar. You can have four quarters, eight eighths, or 16 sixteenth notes. Clap out each bar.

3/4 TIME SIGNATURE

In a bar of 3/4, there are only three quarter beats in the bar. There are many ways of organizing the bar—the last bar of this exercise has a classic waltz beat. Try clapping it.

BASIC PLUCKING

The techniques for plucking the guitar strings are derived from classical music, but you can use them in a whole range of music styles. To build up smooth skills, you should begin with just your thumb and first finger.

FINGER-PICKIN' GOOD

A good hand position leads to accuracy and agility, but there are a couple of different styles of plucking.

Start off with this simple exercise. It gets your fingers used to the feeling of picking individual strings.

classical style—With the guitar on the left leg, the arm has the space to arch around the guitar body. The hand is rounded, relaxed, and away from the strings.

folk style—The guitar is held more horizontally on the right leg and is much tighter to the body. The hand is flatter and closer to the strings, ready to mute them with the palm if needed.

MALAGUEÑA

Malagueña is a traditional Spanish folk tune, based around the chords of E and Am. Start slowly and concentrate on getting the notes right before speeding up.

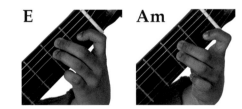

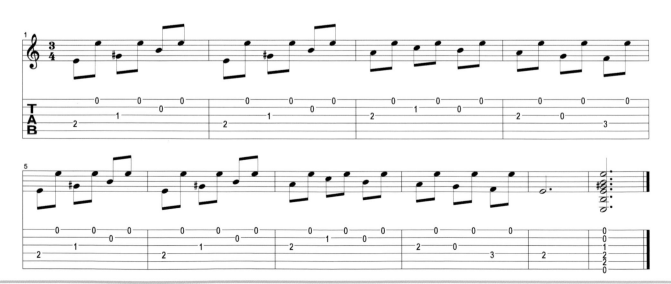

20

PALM MUTING

B y dampening the strings, palm muting stops the notes from ringing out. It may sound like a strange thing to do to a guitar, but this technique adds tension and **dynamics** to your playing.

HOW TO PALM MUTE

Something in the way? When you play palm muted, the guitar makes a thunky, deadened sound. It works particularly well when playing chords with a pick or with country-style fingerpicking.

STEP 1

Rest the base of your playing hand across all the strings, as close to the bridge as possible. Play any note with a pick to hear the effect.

STEP 2

Play a chord with the strings muted. Accent the first few notes to get a really good thunk. Experiment with your hand position and with fingerpicking.

How a note is made

A normal, unmuted note on a guitar is made by plucking the string. This makes the string vibrate. On an acoustic guitar, the vibration of the string is picked up at the bridge. The bridge then makes the soundboard vibrate. This vibration amplifies the sound of a single string. The sound resonating inside the body of the guitar also increases the volume.

Different kinds of strings make different sounds. Classical guitars are strung with soft-sounding nylon strings. Steel-string acoustics use bright-sounding, round-wound steel. Jazz players prefer duller, flat-wound strings.

MAJOR AND MINOR SCALES

The major and minor scales are the two most important systems in Western music. Both scales have an easily recognizable feel, and most tunes are made using the combinations of notes, chords, and harmonies that are found in them.

MAJOR SCALE

Major scales are best for writing a happy or bright-sounding melody.

C MAJOR SCALE

Positions

Because any note can be found on any string, scales and chords can be played in several different positions on the fretboard. The first fret is called 1st position, second fret is 2nd position, and so on.

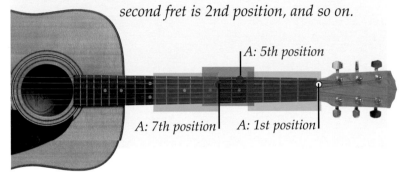

A: 5th position

A: 7th position   *A: 1st position*

NATURAL MINOR SCALE

The **natural** minor scale is a sad-sounding scale. The third sixth and seventh note of the scale have been flattened, or dropped by one fret, or a semitone, to create a darker sound. A minor is the related minor key to C major. Compare the scales to see their similarities and hear their differences.

Top tip

Playing scales is also a really good warm-up activity and a way of increasing your speed on the fretboard.

PLAY-ALONG SONGS

L et's put into practice all the things you have learned so far. Here are three simple melodies to get you working on your chords, single notes, pick-work, and fingerstyle. See if you can guess which melodies are major and which are minor.

MELODIES FOR PLAYING ALONG

Use the melodies below to put everything you have learned into practice. Use a pick, then move on to fingerpicking. Each melody is based around either the major or natural minor scale.

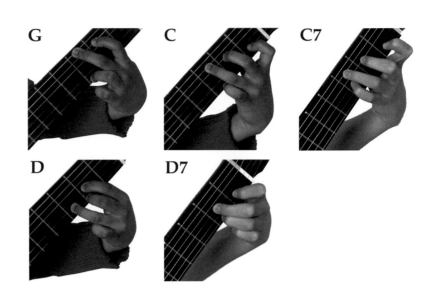

MELODY 23.1

SCARBOROUGH FAIR

A SPOT OF REVISION

One of the best things that you can do when learning an instrument is to review your lessons every now and again. This strengthens your technique and helps things sink in.

CHORD PATTERNS AND MELODIES

With just three chords, such as G major, C major, and D major, you can play a huge number of songs. Try out different combinations of these three chords to see what you come up with—drop in an A minor chord to spice things up a little.

Technical term

chord progression—
A regularly repeating pattern of chords

Here is a melody that uses the chords of G major, C major, and D major.
Play it slowly at first. Concentrate on moving from chords to single notes.

EXERCISE 24.1

HAMMER-ONS

Y ou can add color, depth and range to your playing with a few simple effects. Hammer-ons are one of the most important techniques, helping you to connect notes more smoothly. It is time to take things to the next level.

HAMMER TIME

The hammer-on is a percussive technique—you use your fingers to beat the fingerboard. It helps you play music smoothly, allowing the notes to flow from one to the next. Hammer-ons are key to playing melodies or solos (*see* pages 40–41) and also for playing legato (*see* page 27).

Finger strength

Practicing to get your hammer-ons sounding clean and loud builds up your finger strength. Similarly, practicing scales and chord progressions will also improve finger strength and make your hammer-ons sound much better.

HOW TO HAMMER-ON

STEP 1

Fret the 6th fret on the 1st string with your 1st finger. Pluck it and let it ring.

Hammer-ons in tab

This is how an instruction to hammer on looks like in tablature.

STEP 2

While the note is ringing, swing, or hammer, your 3rd finger down onto the 8th fret (1st string), as forcefully as you can. You should hear the second note sound.

PULL-OFFS

A pull-off is the exact opposite of a hammer-on. Where a hammer-on is used to play an ascending note, pull-offs are for descending runs. Both techniques allow smooth phrasing that cannot be made by picking individual notes.

PULL THE OTHER ONE

Pull-offs don't need as much finger strength as hammer-ons do to make them sound right.

Pull-offs in tab

This is how an instruction to pull-off looks like in tablature.

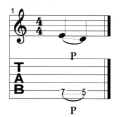

PULL-OFFS TO AN OPEN STRING

STEP 1

Fret the 3rd fret on the 5th string with your 2nd finger. You can use any finger for this, but your 2nd is most often your strongest one. Pluck the string.

STEP 2

While the note is ringing, pull your finger away from the fretboard forcibly, plucking the string with your fretting finger to make the open A note (2nd string) sound. Practice getting the A to sound cleanly.

PULL-OFFS TO A FRETTED STRING

STEP 1

First fret the note on which you want to finish (5th fret, 5th string in this case). Then play the note two frets above (fretted with the 3rd finger).

STEP 2

Pull your 3rd finger off, plucking the string to sound the D note (5th fret, 5th string). Practice adding hammer-ons and pull-offs into a scale (see page 22).

LEGATO AND STACCATO

Both these strange-sounding words are ways of introducing dynamics, shape, and **articulation** into your playing. They are opposites of each other—legato is a smooth and unhurried style, while staccato is choppy and edgy.

SMOOTH LEGATO

Legato connects single notes together, so that they flow with no silence between them. The way to picture legato is like a wave—it always flows without stopping and starting.

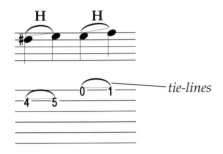

Legato is played using hammer-ons and pull-offs to smooth out the notes, indicated by tie-lines.

CHOPPY STACCATO

Staccato notes have silence in between them. You can picture staccato notes as a line of dots because each dot has a space between them.

Staccato notes are indicated by dots above the notes. Think of playing them as if the guitar strings were red hot.

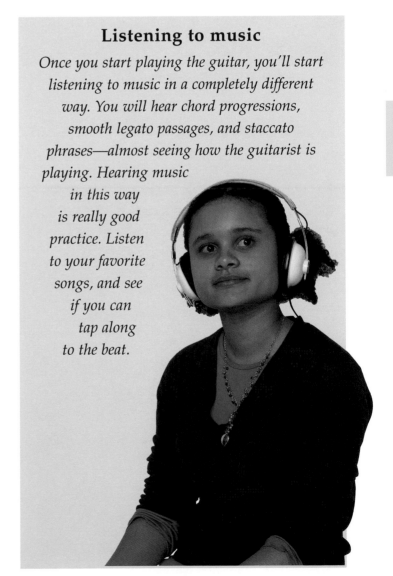

Listening to music

Once you start playing the guitar, you'll start listening to music in a completely different way. You will hear chord progressions, smooth legato passages, and staccato phrases—almost seeing how the guitarist is playing. Hearing music in this way is really good practice. Listen to your favorite songs, and see if you can tap along to the beat.

27

BUILDING UP SPEED

A s you get more confidence and your finger strength improves, you can start increasing the pace at which you play. If you get your basic techniques solid, you will find that speed comes quite easily.

RHYTHM

Page 18 and 19 covered note values and how to count bars of three and four beats. Quarter notes and eighth notes have also been introduced. Next let's cover sixteenth notes, which are twice as fast as eighth notes.

At double the speed you get 16 in a bar of 4/4 (four for each beat).

Thrilling trills

A trill is a fancy turn on a note, made by playing a quick succession of sixteenth-note hammer-ons and pull-offs.

The trill notation   *What you play*

This is what sixteenth notes look like in a 4/4 bar:
EXERCISE 28.1

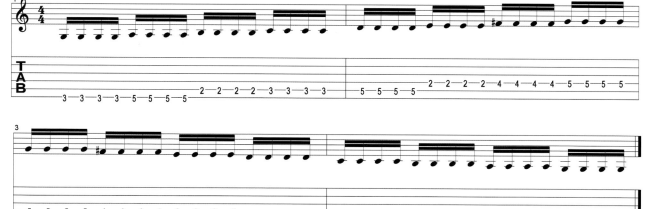

STEP 1

Play along with a metronome to get the feel. Set it to a slow speed of 40 BPM and concentrate on getting the notes to fall on every beat. Practice with a pick.

STEP 2

Increase the speed of the metronome until you can only just get the notes in time. Practice at this speed until it feels easier. Now increase the speed again.

INTERMEDIATE SKILLS

FINGERPICKING

Playing the guitar with your fingers is a versatile technique. All of a sudden you can provide your own rhythm section while floating a melody across the upper register—it sure is fingerpickin' good.

FOLK FINGERSTYLE

Getting the correct hand position is essential for fingerstyle.

STEP 1

Pull your wrist in so that it is flat on the body of the guitar. Your fingers curl over and your thumb is parallel to the strings. This can feel a little strange at first.

STEP 2

Fret a chord and try thumbing the bass notes while picking out the top three notes. Do this until the hand position feels natural. Many players use a thumbpick.

Advanced techniques

Try taking your thumb from behind the neck and hooking it over the top to fret bass notes. Not all players agree with it, but it can be a very useful skill to have.

Here are a couple of examples to get you started with fingerpicking techniques.

EXERCISE 29.1

EXERCISE 29.2

BARRE CHORDS

Barre chords allow you to play chords anywhere on the neck. The shapes are the same ones that you learned as open chords (*see* pages 14–16), but you use your first finger to create a barre (same as a bar) across the guitar's neck.

BARRE TECHNIQUE

Barre chords are named by the shape of the open chord that they imitate. Compare the open E major chord with the E-shape barre chord (right).

E MAJOR (OPEN CHORD)

The nut at the top of the guitar neck forms a barre for the open major chord.

E-SHAPE BARRE CHORD

5th position

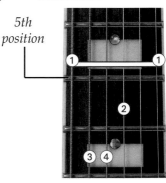

The 1st finger creates a barre, while the rest of the fingers initiate the E shape.

STEP 1

Lay your 1st finger across all the strings. Try to apply even pressure. Your 2nd, 3rd, and 4th fingers form the shape of the open chord.

OTHER BARRE CHORDS

E-MINOR SHAPE

Stick with it

This is one of the biggest steps in learning the guitar and sometimes it can make your fingers sore. Stick with it— before you know it, it becomes second nature.

A-SHAPE

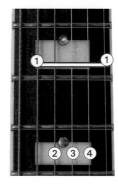

A-MINOR SHAPE

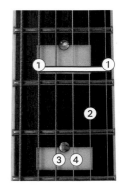

30

INTERMEDIATE SKILLS

POWER CHORDS

These useful chords are partial barre chords, made from their first three notes. Since they do not require a barre, they are much easier to play than a full barre chord. Rock guitarists use them a lot because they can shift between them much more quickly. Compare this type of chord to the barre chords shown on the opposite page.

"A" POWER CHORD

Since they do not contain the third note of the scale, power chords are neither major nor minor.

Practice your **power-chord** techniques with this melody. Pay close attention to the rhythm in bar 5.

EXERCISE 31.1

COMPOSE A MELODY USING BARRE CHORDS

Test out your new knowledge by inventing a song using E-shape and A-shape barre chords. Try to think of chord progressions you have already played in this book. Can you play them as barre chords?

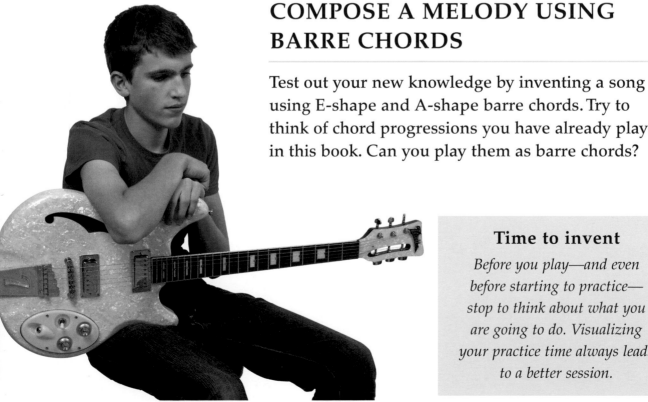

Time to invent

Before you play—and even before starting to practice— stop to think about what you are going to do. Visualizing your practice time always leads to a better session.

MORE SCALES EXERCISES

It is time to revisit the scales. Remember the major scale and natural minor scale on page 22? Well, here are more exercises based on these important scales.

A MAJOR SCALE

Use these scale charts to help you with the exercises.

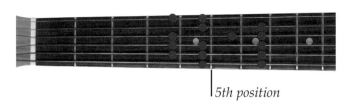

5th position

A MINOR SCALE

5th position

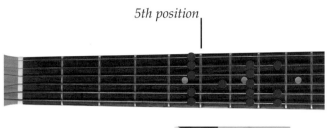

This exercise takes the scale of A major.

EXERCISE 32.1

Your starting position for exercise 32.1.

This exercise takes the scale of A minor.

EXERCISE 32.2

Exercise 32.2 starts at the 7th position.

This exercise mixes both A major and A minor scales.

EXERCISE 32.3

Begin exercise 32.3 on the 10th fret.

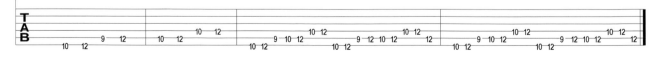

INTERMEDIATE SKILLS

MUSICAL STYLES

No other instrument—except maybe the piano—can play as many different musical styles as the guitar. It really is a chameleon instrument, used in everything from classical to jazz, and Latin to world music.

CLASSICAL AND FLAMENCO

The Spanish guitar, with its small body and nylon strings, is used for classical playing and traditional Latin styles of music, including many types of Latin-American and Caribbean music. The guitar tends to be a rhythm instrument in styles such as bossa nova (Brazilian jazz) or salsa, but a lead instrument for classical compositions. The flamboyant Spanish style called flamenco also uses a classical guitar, with added tap plates on the soundboard for striking.

BLUES AND JAZZ

The steel-string acoustic guitar is the main instrument of blues and jazz, as well as folk and country music. It is often played on its own as a rhythm instrument. Blues players often use their palm to mute the strings (*see* page 21), creating a "shuffle" rhythm.

(*see* page 21)

Many blues guitarists play slide guitar, using a metal or glass slide on the strings to make a wailing or moaning sound.

The arch-top semi-acoustic guitar is a great favorite with jazz musicians for its warm, mellow tones.

PLAY-ALONG SONGS

Well done! You have now battled with barre chords, learned some silky solo skills, and hopefully gained a lot more confidence.

TEST YOUR PLAYING

Below are three exercises for you to practice. Test your progress by sight-reading the tablature or standard notation.

G

SIMPLE FINGERPICKING

This piece is based around the chord of G major. Keep the **tempo** slow and steady.

G MAJOR WORKOUT

This piece will test your fingerpicking skills to the max.

NATURAL MINOR MELODY

This melody starts out in the natural minor key of B, but modulates, or changes, to a major key in the final bar. Listen closely to catch this change.

34

 **D**  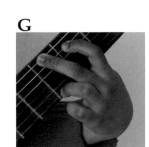 **G** 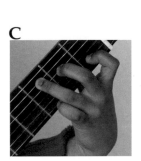  **C**

TOTAL WORKOUT

This piece has it all—chords, single notes, and some crazy rhythms. Set your metronome to a moderate pace, and tap out the beat with your foot.

GET THE GROOVE

Clap out the rhythm. Remember to check the time signature before you start.

The guitar is perfect for playing with friends. You could play these pieces together or try them as rounds, in which each person starts a bar later than the person before.

TRADITIONAL IRISH TUNE

This song should be played at a brisk pace. However, remember to begin slowly and concentrate on getting the notes correct first.

PLAY-ALONG SONGS

BLUES SCALE

Blues is the language of rock 'n' roll. A lot of rock melody lines and tunes can trace their roots back to the blues (*see* page 33), which is based around a very simple scale.

BLUE WITH A FEELIN'

The blues is a form of music which first started in the southern states with the songs of slaves who had been brought from Africa in the 1700s.

Playing the blues is all about feeling. A little technical data is useful for understanding how it works. In the blues scale the third and seventh notes are flattened (down a semitone, or half note—one fret). It is also missing the second and sixth notes where they would be in a normal scale. This makes the blues scale very similar to a minor pentatonic scale (see page 39) but we will come to this later. For now, play the scale below and get the feel of the real blues sound.

Playing with a capo

Playing in another position on the neck, but still want those lovely ringing open chords?

It is a cinch with a capo. This device straps or clamps onto the neck and artificially raises the nut. Where you put it is your choice.

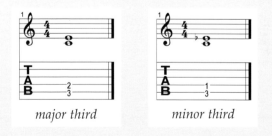

Technical terms

intervals—The space between two notes, measured in length up the scale (1 – 8)

major and minor thirds—A minor third is flattened by a semitone. Compare its sound to a major third by playing one after the other.

major third   *minor third*

BLUESY SOUNDS

Follow this scale up and down the fretboard. Start slowly before building up the tempo.

ADVANCED SKILLS

ALTERNATE PICKING

By now, you will be getting pretty handy at using a pick. You should know how to strum chords and be a master at playing scales with one. Here is a technique that will increase your speed and accuracy with the pick.

EASY PICKINGS

It's hard work picking a string in one direction all the time, especially on solos. Alternate picking is a great way to pick each string at a higher tempo. It is more accurate and should be used all the time. It is extremely useful when it comes to soloing or fast riffs.

Walking fingers

Another picking technique is to walk the first two fingers on a string. You can extend this technique to play arpeggios. These are chords in which each note of the chord is sounded on its own, one after the other.

STEP 1

First start picking a certain note on any string. Pick the string firmly downwards, but stop the pick as soon as it has plucked the string.

STEP 2

The next stroke is upward. Continue playing an alternating down-up-down on the string, making sure to make the strokes even. Practice with a metronome.

Start this alternate picking exercise slowly. Increase the tempo when you feel comfortable.

EXERCISE 37.1

MAJOR PENTATONIC SCALE

The pentatonic scale is made up of five notes taken from a standard eight-note octave. The major pentatonic scale is a lot like the major scale (*see* page 22), but the fourth and seventh intervals are taken out. If you already know the major scale, finding your major pentatonic scale is simple.

Learn your scales

It may feel like a chore, but scales are the building blocks of tunes. Knowing your scales helps you pick out a tune on the guitar and solo like nobody's business.

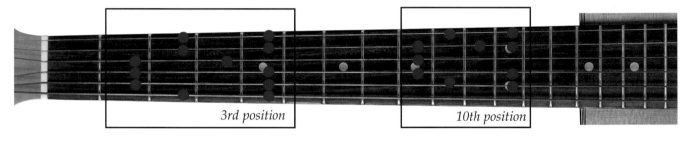

3rd position   *10th position*

This melody is based on the A major pentatonic scale.

EXERCISE 38.1

MINOR PENTATONIC SCALE

The minor pentatonic scale is the jewel in the crown of scales in the guitar world. Based on the natural minor scale (*see* page 22)—with added flattened third and seventh notes—this is the scale used in most rock and blues solos.

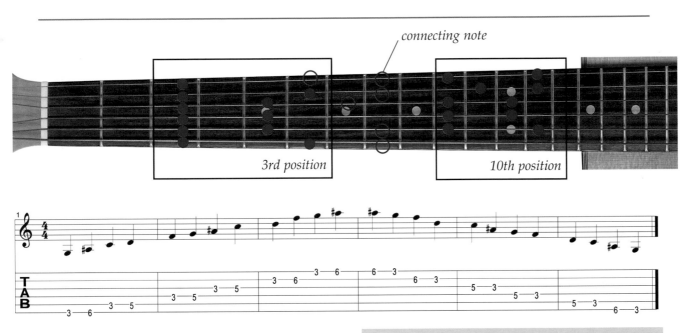

connecting note

3rd position

10th position

Compare this to the blues scale on page 36. You'll find a lot of similarities.

Soloing

Mastering this scale in all positions is important if you want to improvise, or make music up as you go along, in rock and blues music. Practice changing positions with runs that use the connecting notes (above).

B

Here is a melody based on the minor pentatonic scale. You should also try and construct your own melody.

EXERCISE 39.1

SOLOING TECHNIQUES

Playing guitar as a solo instrument is really fun, whether you are playing red-hot lead lines on an electric or blistering runs on the classical guitar. There is a whole range of techniques and effects that you can use when playing solos to increase your speed, dexterity, and flashiness.

CONTROLLED BENDS

At first you might find that you need all three fingers to bend a string.

Bending a string makes the pitch of the note rise. It is used to travel from one note to another smoothly. Pluck a fretted string and, while it is still ringing, push the string up toward your head. Practice hitting the notes one fret and two frets above the starting note.

PLAYING RIFFS

Practice! Practice! Practice!

It's no lie—practice is the only way to improve your playing. If you want to be really good, you are going to have to put in the time.

Many rock solos and melody lines are built around repeating riffs. One useful technique is to fret the top part of chords on the 1st, 2nd, and 3rd strings in the upper positions above the 12th fret. Drag the pick down across the strings while using your 3rd and 4th finger to add passing notes, or string bends.

VIBRATO

STEP 1

Vibrato makes a note sing by pulsing its pitch. It is made by wobbling the fretting finger. Play a note, then push the hand forward of the finger.

STEP 2

Quickly swing the hand back, moving from the wrist, and repeat. Can you hear the singing sound?

SLIDE

A slide is a quick way to reach a note during fast runs. If a note is one, two, or even more frets above the one you are playing, simply slide your fingers up the neck to reach it.

HARMONICS

STEP 1

The natural harmonics of a guitar are the pure tones of the strings, without any overtones. Touch any string lightly, directly above the 12th fret.

STEP 2

Pluck the string and release your finger from it at the same time. The first harmonic will ring out. You will find other harmonics at the 5th and 7th frets.

Artificial harmonics

The natural harmonics of a string are the places that an open string will produce harmonic tones. You can create artificial, or forced, harmonics on a fretted string by placing the heel of your picking hand on the strings 12 frets above the fretted note and plucking.

BLUES MELODIES

Now you have learned all about scales, soloing techniques, intervals, and major and minor thirds. It's time to enjoy yourself. Kick back, relax, and play some of the songs on these two pages. You're nearly there.

PLAYING THE BLUES

The chord progression in the piece below is typical of blues music. It goes from the 1st note of the scale to a chord based around the 4th note. Then it goes to a chord based around the 5th note of the scale, before returning to the 1st. Check out the blues scale on page 36.

12-BAR BLUES

Below is a 12-bar blues melody in a 4/4 time signature. The first three bars consist of bluesy chords, and the next three bars consist of a melody that you can follow. This will put the blues scale into practice.

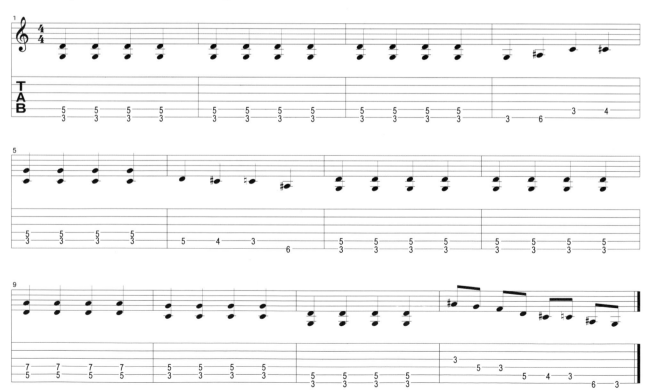

ROCK MELODIES

Congratulations! You have finished your lessons. By now you should at least have a firm grasp of the basics. Practice the techniques often, and use this book as reference, flipping back when you need a refresher on something.

PLAY ALONG

Rock melodies are often based around eight-bar blocks. Here are two for you to try. The first play-along song is made up of power chords. Feel free to change them around and make your own melody. On the right are all the chords you will need.

POWER CHORDS

POWER CHORDS ROCK

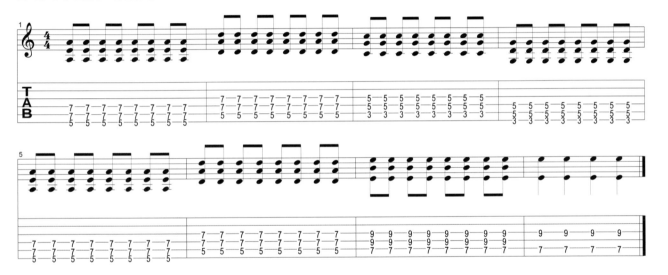

RIFFING ON THE MINOR PENTATONIC

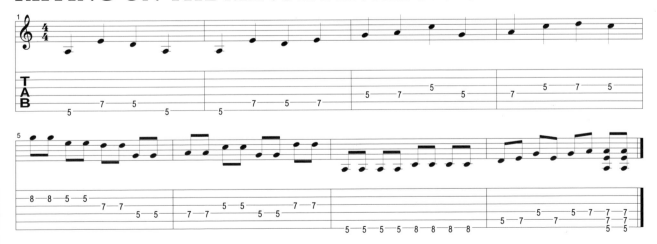

SIGNIFICANT PLAYERS

Y ou could write a whole book on great guitar players. Here are just a few of those glittering stars who have lit up the world of music and changed guitar-playing and guitars forever.

SIX-STRING LEGENDS

The twentieth century was the era when the guitar came into its own as an instrument. As the steel-string guitar grew in popularity, it became a cheap instrument to own and was easy to carry around. People would use it for accompaniment when they got together to sing. Later, with the invention of the electric pickup, the guitar was transformed into a solo instrument. The six-string gradually became the center of musical combos, and the guitar player was the star.

Charlie Christian

There were other guitar players around who used the new electric pickup to amplify their sound, but it was Charlie Christian who turned the guitar into a solo instrument. Once a backing instrument only in the largest jazz bands, the six-string was now loud enough to be a lead instrument like the saxophone. Nobody had ever heard a style like Christian's, when he played with the Benny Goodman Quintet. He also pioneered a new style called bebop jazz.

DJANGO REINHARDT

Django Reinhardt was a master of the acoustic guitar. Born in Belgium to a traveling family, he grew up on the road and played Spanish-influenced jazz in Paris! When he was 18, his hands were burned so badly in a fire that he could only play with his first two fingers. Instead of giving up, Django invented his own way of playing.

Although he couldn't read or write, Reinhardt amazed more refined guitarists, such as Andrés Segovia, with his playing technique, often making up or improvising melodies as he went along. His guitar group, Quintet de Hot Club de Paris, was certainly the hottest thing in Paris in the 1920s and '30s.

BLUES

Jazz was the pop music of the 1920s, '30s and '40s. The blues was more of a folksy kind of music. Rock 'n' roll burst on the scene in the 1950s, using lots of sped-up blues tunes. Slowly, the simple, heartfelt melodies and rhythms of blues became more popular.

MUDDY WATERS

McKinley "Muddy Waters" Morganfield was a blues musician who had a huge influence on young guitar players in the 1960s. People had never heard such music with its loud amplified guitars and thunderous beat.

JIMI HENDRIX

Nobody before had ever played guitar like Jimi Hendrix. A fantastically talented blues soloist, Jimi's guitar work soared. He often played with his teeth, set fire to his guitar, and even smashed it up. A left-handed player, Hendrix was known for playing a right-handed Fender Stratocaster, with the strings strung upside down.

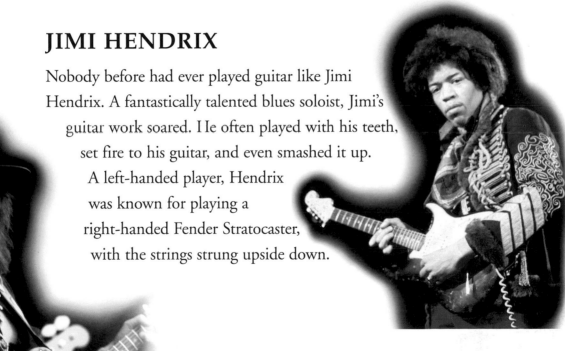

STEVIE RAY VAUGHAN

Stevie Ray Vaughan got his first guitar at age seven—a toy with only three strings. He learned to play using this guitar and eventually became one of the world's most influential blues guitarists. Vaughan was famous for his battered 1963 Fender Stratocaster— his favorite—which he had found in an old music shop.

LONG LIVE ROCK 'N' ROLL

As the 1960s rolled on, guitar music changed again, entering the era of rock. Technology improved, and bands were now able to play louder and rock harder. The age of superstar guitar heroes was born.

JIMMY PAGE

Perhaps the ultimate rock god, Jimmy Page was the guitarist for the British band Led Zeppelin—the first world-famous heavy rock band. As well as a blistering soloist, Page was a very good folk musician. He often sprinkled his music with melody lines played on a 12-string guitar. He was also famous for playing his electric guitar with a violin bow. His trademark guitar was a double-necked Gibson SG (left).

ANGUS YOUNG

Dressed in schoolboy's clothes, you can't miss Angus Young, the guitarist for the rock band AC/DC. His high-energy style of guitar playing is hard-rocking and hard-riffing, using a lot of stripped-down power chords. As well as possessing great skill and speed, Young twists the blues to get melody-rich, emotional guitar solos. On stage, he goes crazy, running and rolling around while playing solos.

POP-TASTIC POP-PICKERS

While rock guitar moved to the front of a band, pop guitarists tended to remain in the background—but still with great effect.

THE BEATLES

The Beatles were the most successful band ever. This Liverpool band started playing straight rhythm and blues, before changing pop music forever in the late 1960s. As well as killer melodies, John Lennon and George Harrison cleverly mixed their guitar parts, to create complex, catchy rhythms. Harrison complemented this with his sweet, country-influenced solos.

BRIAN MAY

Queen are the second-most successful band of all time. Guitarist Brian May played off singer Freddie Mercury's theatrical singing with grand guitar solos, using lots of effects. May plays a guitar that he built himself with the help of his dad.

47

Custom-made guitar

The singer and guitarist Prince is one of the most talented, virtuosic pop performers. He mixes a huge range of styles in his playing—usually playing his own custom-made guitars.

ANDRÉS SEGOVIA

It's not all just about rock, pop, and jazz guitar, though—while the rock revolution was going on, certain musicians distinguished themselves as classical masters. One such guitarist was Andrés Segovia. His expressive style and clever reinterpreting of classical pieces brought this beautiful form of music to many people. Segovia also did a lot to encourage beginners to play the guitar.

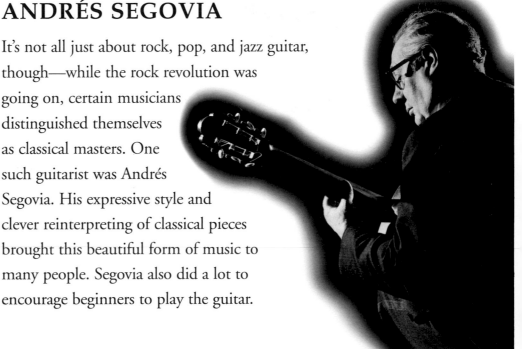

GLOSSARY

apoyando Plucking note, also called the rest stroke

arpeggio A broken chord, in which the notes are played in sequence

articulation The manner in which notes are played

barre chord A chord with the finger used as a 'barre' across the fretboard

deaden To make less intense, sensitive, or vigorous

dynamics How loud or quiet the music should be played

fills Improvisations at the end of musical phrases

key signatures How many sharps and flats in a piece

legato Played smoothly

metronome A device that marks time by ticking or flashing at adjustable intervals

natural A symbol to indicate that the original note should be played

octave The interval of eight diatonic degrees between two tones of the same name

open chord A chord played with open strings ringing

plectrum A plastic pick for strumming strings

position The fret number

power chord A three-finger chord

riff A repeating pattern, often used as a foundation in rock songs

staccato Detached notes, played with a punch

strumming Brushing the strings with a plectrum, or a thumb, or thumbnail

tempo The pace of music; how fast or slow it goes

time signature How many beats in a bar, and of which type

tirando A plucking stroke, also called the free stroke

tonic The main, and first, note of a scale or key signature; also called the root note

INDEX